Martina Munzittu

Recipes

from Italian Friends and Family

First published in Great Britain in 2014
by ESSENZA Publishing
Copyright © Martina Munzittu 2014

The author's moral rights have been asserted.
All rights reserved. No part of this publication may be
reproduced, stored in a retrieval system or transmitted in any
form or by any means, electronic, mechanical, photocopying
or otherwise, without the prior permission of the publisher.

ISBN 978-0-9928807-0-5

Notes
- All spoon and cup measurements are level unless otherwise specified.
- Uncooked or partly cooked eggs should not be served to the very old or frail, the very young or to pregnant women.

Designer and Art Director Janet Tallon, Freakettona
Commissioning Editor and Food Stylist Martina Munzittu

Contents

Introduction	5
What is tiramisu made of?	6
Frequently Asked Questions	8
The recipes	11
Giulia's Traditional Tiramisu	12
Anna's Limoncello Tiramisu	14
Claudia's Tiramisu Light	16
Monica's Coconut Tiramisu	19
Cristina's Fun Tiramisu Cakes	20
Dalia's Tiramisu Cups	24
Dalia's Tiramisu Cupcakes	26
Dalia's Tiramisu Cheesecake	29
Laura's Banana Tiramisu	31
Rita's Pineapple Tiramisu	32
Rita's Orange Tiramisu	34
Manuela's Tiramisu Brownie	37
Ferruccio's Tiramisu Cake	39
Mariangela's Strawberry Tiramisu	42
Rita's Tiramisu Pancakes	44
Martina's Chocolate Tiramisu	46
Martina's Lemon Curd Tiramisu	48
Maria Grazia's Baileys Tiramisu	50
Martina's Tiramisu Ice Cream	53
Maria Antonietta's Gluten-Free Tiramisu	54
Tiziana's Peach Tiramisu	56
Sofia's Rainbow Tiramisu	58
Mamma's Panettone Tiramisu	60
Brunella's Tiramisu Coffee	63
Cristina's Vegan Tiramisu	64
Tiramisu disasters	66
Tiramisu party	76
Acknowledgements	94
About Martina Munzittu	95
Index	96

Introduction

A few months ago, one Saturday morning, I was making tiramisu for some friends who were coming to dinner. Over the years I have changed the traditional recipe and added a layer of chocolate mousse to it.
I love espresso coffee, but I'm not fond of coffee in my desserts, so I have also replaced the coffee with Martini. While I was melting the chocolate in the saucepan, I started to think of the many times I tried tiramisu as a guest in the homes of my friends and relatives in Italy. How a simple, wonderful dessert could taste quite different depending on the person who made it. I remembered how, over time, I had tried some variations of the classic version, but had also had fruity tiramisus during the summer, sampled children's ones at birthday parties and tasted more sophisticated treats on special occasions.

That's how this book was born. I asked my friends and family in Italy to give me their tiramisu recipes so I could share them with you. Not only that, I also asked them to make their tiramisu and take a photo. So, unlike many photos in food publications and other recipe books, the pictures that you see next to these recipes have been taken in a real kitchen by the person who made the dessert, just before they ate it!
Since great cooks are not always great photographers, you will probably find that the taste of these recipes will surpass their artistic merit. The list of tiramisus in this book is by no means exhaustive. However, there are twenty-five recipes which should cater for a wide range of tastes. We have: alcoholic and fruity versions; tiramisu cakes, cheesecake and cupcakes; classic tiramisu; egg-free and gluten-free desserts; low-fat and low-sugar tiramisu; children's tiramisus; ice-cream and pancakes; and many more.
I have prepared and enjoyed every one of these desserts. The majority are really easy to make, and I hope you will try quite a few. These tiramisus have been made by ordinary people like you and me; you can find out a little bit about them after each recipe. I am no chef or food professional; I just have a passion for food and a sweet tooth!

A brief history

Whom do we have to thank for the existence of tiramisu?
This wonderful dessert was invented by Roberto Linguanotto, in the early 1970s. He was a chef at the popular restaurant Alle Beccherie in Treviso (Veneto), and was once asked to prepare a **dolce della casa**, a house dessert that would work for both adults and children. So he came up with **tiramesù**, which was the original name in the local dialect.
The dessert proved to be very popular with the customers of the restaurant and soon became known in Italian as tiramisù, which means 'pick me up', or 'cheer me up'.
I am sure we can appreciate why this choice of name is so appropriate, as it has turned out to be the most popular Italian dessert in the world.

What is tiramisu made of?

The main ingredients of a classic tiramisu are mascarpone cheese, eggs, sugar, espresso coffee and sponge fingers/ladyfingers.

Eggs – it's very important to use fresh eggs. There's a debate as to whether to use the whole egg or just the yolk. The original recipe by Linguanotto only used the egg yolks; some recipes in this book use the whole egg, some only half the whites. The whipped egg white creates more volume in the mascarpone mousse, giving it a lighter consistency. If you want to have a rich mousse, you can reduce the number of egg whites, or omit them entirely. When in a recipe I say 'discard the egg whites' I don't mean throw them away. I simply mean do not include them. You can use those egg whites in other ways, such as for making meringues, crepes or omelettes, for instance.

Egg whites will whisk to a greater volume when they are at room temperature than when chilled, so always remove the eggs from the fridge at least half an hour before you start preparing your dessert. Take great care when you separate the whites from the yolks, as there must not be any trace of yolk left in them, otherwise they will not whip properly. The egg yolks and sugar need to be whisked for several minutes, until you obtain a light and airy mousse. Remember: because tiramisu is made with raw eggs, there's always a very small risk of food poisoning.

Mascarpone – this dairy product is the real deal. I have been served tiramisus made with cream instead, but they're not convincing. If you want to try other dairy products for a healthier alternative (ricotta or low-fat yogurt for instance), then that's OK but do not use cream instead of mascarpone. It will not taste the same. Mascarpone is normally kept in the fridge, but leave it at room temperature for at least 30 minutes before making your tiramisu, as it needs to soften a little.

Sponge fingers (ladyfingers) or sponge cake – the sponge fingers in Italian are called *savoiardi*. The role of both, sponge fingers and sponge cake, is to be dipped in the liquid (coffee or liqueur) and then placed in the serving dish. The mascarpone mousse is usually spread over the sponge fingers. I recommend you buy sponge fingers/ladyfingers made in Italy, if you can. Most supermarkets in the UK and America seem to import them these days. The reason I suggest this is because the non-Italian sponge fingers, which are often used for trifles, tend to be much drier and thinner and they will not soak up the liquid in the right way, resulting in a disastrous tiramisu.

Sugar – always use white sugar unless the recipe specifies otherwise. I prefer caster sugar, but granulated sugar works well too.

Espresso coffee if you don't have an espresso machine, you can use a *Moka caffettiera* (like the one in the picture). I have never used any other type of coffee for tiramisu, so I can't guarantee what it will taste like if you use instant coffee. If you like your coffee sweet, I suggest you sweeten your coffee to taste before you dip your sponge fingers in it.

Other liquids for dipping – you can have alcohol such as Martini, Baileys, Cointreau, Rum, Amaretto, Brandy or Vinsanto. If you like strong alcoholic flavours, you can use them neat. However, they can be overpowering, especially if the sponge fingers are well soaked. Most of my friends and I prefer to dilute the liquid 50 per cent alcohol, 50 per cent water. It's up to your personal taste and that of your guests. You can use fruit juice for the fruity tiramisus, and there is no need to dilute the juice. The temperature of the liquid is important too. If you use coffee, you must let it cool down, and if you go for fruit juice, it must not be straight from the fridge.

The sponge fingers will soak up the liquids better when they are lukewarm. The quantities of liquid in the recipes are a rough guide. Depending on how long you dip your sponge fingers in the liquid, you may end up with some liquid left at the end, or you may run out before you finish. However, we're talking small quantities here. If you run out, just make up some more. If you have too much liquid unused, it may mean that your sponge fingers have not absorbed enough and may be a little dry. If this happens, do not panic: there's nothing you can do at this stage so just enjoy your dessert when the time comes. It's a lesson learnt for when you make it again. So the big question is: how long do you dip the sponge fingers for? I'd say turn them around in the liquid for 3-4 seconds; they need to become moist but not soggy.

Cocoa powder and chocolate – the traditional tiramisu has bitter cocoa powder dusted on top of each layer. An alternative is to use grated plain chocolate, with at least 70 per cent cocoa. It's important to buy good quality chocolate; I use Lindt chocolate. The difference between cocoa and chocolate is the crunching effect when you savour that lovely mascarpone mousse, although the cocoa powder gives it a more velvety texture. If in doubt, try both.

Frequently Asked Questions

How long in advance do I need to make my tiramisu?
Tiramisu needs to be kept in the fridge for at least four hours, once it's been prepared. If you're making it for a dinner party in the evening, I recommend you make it in the morning and refrigerate it straight away. However, in my opinion, the dessert reaches its peak on the second day, so you could make it the day before you plan to have it.

How long will tiramisu last?
Up to three days, but it must always be kept in the fridge. If I make my tiramisu on a Saturday morning, for instance, it will last until Tuesday (assuming we haven't eaten it all before!).

Can you freeze tiramisu?
Yes. It's best to freeze it as fresh as possible. For instance, if you make it on a Monday, and you find that half of it wasn't consumed, it's best to freeze it then, rather than freeze it two days later. You must defrost it thoroughly before eating it.

My mascarpone mousse is too runny; what can I do?
Take some whipping cream from the fridge and whip it into stiff peaks. Gently fold it into the mousse. This will help to thicken it.

My mascarpone mousse is too dense/rich; how can I make it lighter?
Take a couple of egg whites and beat them into stiff peaks. Gently fold them into the mousse. This will help to make it airy and lighter. If you want the mousse simply to be more liquid, just add a little milk.

How many layers of sponge fingers and mousse should a tiramisu have?
This depends on the size of your serving dish and personal taste. It's up to you. Some people prefer to have only one layer of sponge fingers and two layers of mousse, some

prefer to have one of each. There are no strict rules. It also depends on the quantities of the mousse and of the other ingredients.

What tools/equipment do I need to make a classic tiramisu?
Three bowls to start with. Use a large one for whisking the egg yolks with the sugar; this will eventually contain the rest of the mixture (mascarpone and egg whites). You will also need a medium bowl for beating the egg whites and a smaller bowl for your coffee (or other liquid) for dipping your sponge fingers in. You will need a serving dish, or cups if you decide to present your dessert in single portions. To prepare the mascarpone mousse you will need a whisk (an electric whisk will get the job done quicker) and a wooden spoon. Once the mousse is ready, it will come in handy to have a ladle or large spoon ready to spread it over your sponge fingers. A small, fine strainer will be needed for dusting cocoa powder over your tiramisu.

Should the tiramisu be served straight from the fridge?
No. It's best to remove the dessert from the fridge at least 20 minutes before serving it.

THE RECIPES

Giulia's Traditional Tiramisu

Serves 6–8

5 eggs
250 g (9 oz) [1¼ cups] sugar
500 g (1 lb 2 oz) [2 cups] mascarpone
300 ml (½ pint) [1¼ cups] espresso coffee
300 g sponge fingers/ladyfingers - they usually come in 200 g (7 oz) packs
Unsweetened cocoa powder

1. Separate the eggs, placing all the yolks in one bowl and the whites of 3 eggs in another bowl. Discard 2 egg whites.
2. Whisk the yolks with the sugar until you get a light, pale mousse.
3. Add the mascarpone, and mix until you obtain a smooth cream.
4. Beat the egg whites until they form stiff peaks.
5. With a wooden spoon, fold the egg whites into the mascarpone mousse, with slow movements, working from the bottom of the bowl upwards.
6. Choose a serving dish for your tiramisu.
7. Line the bottom of the dish with a layer of half of the sponge fingers.
8. Pour some coffee over the sponge fingers, enough to moisten them, but not to soak them completely.
9. Place a layer of mascarpone mousse over the sponge fingers.
10. Dip the remaining biscuits in the coffee and put another layer over the mousse.
11. Cover the biscuits with another layer of mascarpone mousse.
12. Dust the top with cocoa powder.
13. Refrigerate for four hours before serving.

Suggestions: the traditional tiramisu recipe uses cocoa powder, but sometimes Giulia prefers to use grated plain chocolate to decorate the dessert. The quantities for this tiramisu will fit a dish of 22 x 25 cm (8½ x 10 inches), with two sponge finger layers. But it's important to remember that you can have as many layers as you want. You could have a smaller dish with three layers, or a larger dish with one layer. You might also like to serve this tiramisu in single glass cups.

My friend Giulia Beyman lives in Rome with her husband, her young son and a family of seven adventurous cats. She writes mystery books with a hint of romance. Her novels A Cry in the Shadows and Words in the Dark are available in Italian and English. Giulia loves animals, yoga and cinema. She adores reading various genres and she collects books at every opportunity. She finds knitting very relaxing, but she can't find enough time to spend on this lovely activity. When it comes to cooking, Giulia loves simple recipes and healthy eating, and prefers to use locally produced food. Her favourite dessert is Mont Blanc: a meringue with whipped cream and sweetened chestnuts.

Anna's Limoncello Tiramisu

Serves 6–8

250 g (9 oz) [1 cup] mascarpone
200 ml (7 fl oz) [¾ cup] limoncello
250 ml (9 fl oz) [1 cup] whipping cream
4 eggs
300 g sponge fingers/ladyfingers (they usually come in 200 g (7 oz) packs
350 ml (12 fl oz) [1½ cups] water
325 g (11½ oz) [1½ cups] sugar
1 organic lemon

1. Place 175 g (6 oz) [¾ cup] of sugar in a saucepan with the water and bring to the boil. Let it boil for 2–3 minutes then turn off the heat and leave it to cool down.
2. Grate the lemon zest into a small bowl.
3. Place the remaining sugar in a bowl. Add 2 whole eggs, the yolks of 2 eggs and the lemon zest. Discard the remaining 2 egg whites.
4. Whisk the eggs with the sugar and lemon zest until you obtain a light, pale mousse.
5. Add the mascarpone and whisk again.
6. Add 120 ml (4 fl oz) [½ cup] of limoncello and stir in with a wooden spoon.
7. In a separate bowl whip the cream into stiff peaks; add it to the egg mixture and stir to combine. Your mascarpone/limoncello mousse is ready.
8. When the sugary water has cooled down, add the rest of the limoncello. Stir.
9. Place this syrup in a bowl.
10. Choose the serving dish for your tiramisu. The one in the photo is 20 x 25 cm (8 x 10 inches).
11. Place a layer of limoncello mousse at the bottom of your dish.
12. Dip the sponge fingers in the syrup; let them soak enough on each side to become moist but not soggy.
13. Place a layer of sponge fingers on top of the mousse.
14. Add another layer of mousse.
15. Repeat with another layer of sponge fingers dipped in syrup.
16. Finish with a layer of mousse on the top.
17. Refrigerate for four hours before serving.

Anna Maria Serra is my friend Valentina's mum. They both live in Teulada, a town southwest of Sardinia. Valentina has prepared a lovely pasta sauce recipe for my other book, but when we were talking about this book, she recommended I try her mum's Limoncello Tiramisu and I wasn't disappointed. The limoncello she used in this recipe was made by Anna herself, using lemons that came from their own citrus fruit orchard. Anna used to be a professional chef; for work she mostly cooked savoury dishes, but at home she loved to prepare sweet treats for her family. Now that she's retired, she spends some of her time looking after her grandchildren. She also enjoys embroidery and the art of making the traditional Sardinian costume, specifically the one from Teulada.
Her favourite dessert is semifreddo al mirto: a sponge cake with crème pâtissière and myrtle berries.

Claudia's Tiramisu Light

Here's a guilt-free version of this luxury dessert. Claudia's Tiramisu is not only low in fat, but is also low in sugar. It might also appeal to people who are into raw food cuisine.

Serves 4

Ingredients for the base
100 g (3½ oz) [½ cup] almonds, shelled but not peeled
5 dates
1 tablespoon of lemon zest
2 tablespoons of espresso coffee

Ingredients for the mousse
300 g (10 oz) [1¼ cups] ricotta
2 eggs
5 tablespoons of Stevia*

1. Place all the ingredients for the base in a food processor and blend until you obtain a smooth mixture.
2. Should the mixture appear dry, add a little more coffee. It should have a smooth consistency, but not be runny.
3. Divide the mixture between 4 cups or small bowls.
4. Refrigerate.
5. Separate the egg yolks from the whites and place them in different bowls.
6. Whisk the egg yolks with the Stevia until you obtain a smooth cream.
7. Add the ricotta and mix with a wooden spoon until you get a mousse with no lumps.
8. Add a pinch of salt to the egg whites and beat them into stiff peaks.
9. With a wooden spoon, gently fold the egg whites into the mousse, working from the bottom of the bowl.
10. Divide the mousse between the cups or bowls.
11. If you wish, you can sprinkle some grated plain chocolate on top as decoration.
12. Refrigerate for four hours before serving.

Suggestions: as an alternative to coffee you could use one or two tablespoons of almond milk. Ricotta can be replaced by low fat Greek yogurt. If you have an allergy to almonds, you can make a base with 100 g (3½ oz) crushed biscuits. In the UK you might like to use Rich Tea biscuits; in America you can buy the Italian Pavesini biscuits. They are both light and low in calories.

*Stevia is a South American herb that has been used as a natural sweetener for centuries. It has no calories, and it's much sweeter than sugar. It's often sold under different brands and packaging, but it should be clear that it's Stevia leaf.

My friend Claudia Peduzzi lives in Domodossola, an alpine town north of Milan. Claudia is an architect and, as well as being quite gifted with languages (she speaks Italian, German, English and French), she's an avid reader who goes through an average of five books a month. She not only reads books, but she also reviews them. As if that were not enough, she has a passion for knitting, crochet and cross-stitch. She doesn't buy presents for friends; she actually makes gifts for them with her own hands. Claudia is vegetarian; she loves cooking and experimenting with new recipes. She's a fitness and well-being fanatic, hence her own version of a healthy tiramisu. I couldn't have come up with this, so I'm really grateful that someone did.
Claudia's favourite dessert is ice cream.

Monica's Coconut Tiramisu

1. Separate the yolks from the egg whites and place them in different bowls.
2. Whisk the egg yolks with the sugar until you obtain a light, pale mousse.
3. Add the mascarpone and whisk.
4. In a third bowl, whip the cream into stiff peaks. Add the cream to the mascarpone mousse and mix with a spoon.
5. Add a pinch of salt to the egg whites and beat them into stiff peaks.
6. Fold the egg whites into the mixture with a wooden spoon, with gentle circular movements.
7. Add three-quarters of the desiccated coconut to the mousse and mix gently with a wooden spoon.
8. Pour the coffee into a small bowl.
9. Pour the liqueur into another small bowl.
10. Choose your serving dish. The one in the photo is 30 cm (12 inches) in diameter.
11. Place a layer of coconut mousse on the bottom of the dish.
12. Sprinkle with cocoa powder or grated chocolate and some coconut flakes.
13. Dip the sponge fingers into the coffee: you can turn them around two or three times. They must not soak up too much, yet they must absorb some of the liquid.
14. Lay the sponge fingers on top of the mousse.
15. Place another layer of mousse over the sponge fingers.
16. Sprinkle with cocoa powder or grated chocolate. Add more coconut flakes.
17. Dip the sponge fingers into the liqueur for 3–4 seconds and line the dish with them.
18. Finish with a layer of mousse.
19. Decorate the top with cocoa powder or grated chocolate and coconut flakes.
20. Refrigerate for four hours before serving.

Suggestions: you don't have to have coffee and liqueur in this dessert. You can have either one or the other, if you prefer.

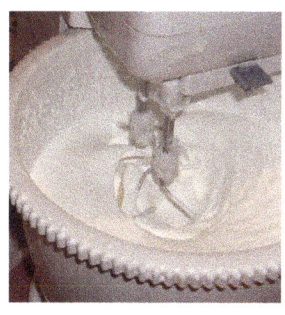

Serves 8–10

500 g sponge fingers/ladyfingers - they usually come in 200 g (7 oz) packs
500 g (1 lb 2 oz) [2 cups] mascarpone
250 g (9 fl oz) [1 cup] whipping cream
4 eggs
4 tablespoons sugar
250 ml (9 fl oz) [1 cup] coffee
250 ml (9 fl oz) [1 cup] Vermouth or Maraschino liquor
200 g (7 oz) [2⅓ cups] desiccated coconut
Unsweetened cocoa powder or plain chocolate

Monica Loi lives in Decimomannu, a town north of Cagliari, Sardinia. We've been friends since high school. She's the Vice-Commander of the Police in Villacidro, which happens to be her home town. It is renowned for its mountains and beautiful landscapes. Monica loves to go walking in the hills, exploring nature and taking photos of the wild flowers and streams. She's a keen gardener and has a passion for cacti and any plant that reminds her of the desert. She's into DIY – her toolbox beats any of her friends' (and we're talking guys here) – and she's pretty good at restoring antique furniture. Monica is not only a career woman, but also a home-maker; she has two children, who are now grown up. Monica is a great cook. She's prepared some lovely risotto and pasta sauce recipes for my other books, and she's into making jams, pickles and other treats. Her favourite dessert is zuppa inglese: it's similar to tiramisu, but the sponge fingers are generally dipped in liqueur and the cream is a crème pâtissière.

Cristina's Fun Tiramisu Cakes

Here is an alternative tiramisu cake shaped like an animal. You have a ladybird/ladybug, a mouse and a hedgehog. How do you achieve that dome shape? You take a bowl, line the inside with strips of sponge cake, spread a layer of mascarpone mousse on top and then you add another layer of sponge cake, and so on, until you gradually fill the bowl up, layer after layer. You turn the bowl upside down and there you have it, a delicious dome-shaped cake.

Serves 10–12 children (or 8 adults)

These are the ingredients for a bowl measuring 22 cm (8½ inches) in diameter. If you use a different size bowl, you need to adjust the quantities. The form of the bowl is perfect for the ladybird. The hedgehog and the mouse have a slight oval shape; you can obtain that by placing some creased tinfoil on two opposite sides of the bowl, trying to flatten the curve of the bowl a little. The mouse in the picture was made with a bowl measuring 10 cm (4 inches) in diameter, so with these quantities you would make two mice.

Making the sponge cake

1. Separate the egg whites from the yolks and place them in different bowls.
2. Add half the sugar to the yolks and whisk for several minutes until light and fluffy.
3. Add the other half of the sugar to the egg whites and beat them into stiff peaks.
4. Sieve a third of the flour into the bowl with the egg yolks. Mix with a wooden spoon.
5. Fold part of the egg whites into the mixture.
6. Sieve another third of the flour and mix with a wooden spoon.
7. Fold in some more of the egg whites.
8. Sieve the remaining flour into the mixture. Stir.
9. Gently incorporate the rest of the egg whites until you have a smooth mixture.
10. Grease the baking tray with butter and dust with flour.
11. Place in the oven at 180°C (350° F) [Gas Mark 4] for 40 minutes. You can check if your cake is ready by inserting a thin skewer in the middle. If it comes out clean, your cake is done.

Making the mascarpone mousse

1. Separate the egg whites from the yolks. Discard the whites.
2. Whisk the egg yolks with the sugar until you get a light, pale mousse.
3. Add the mascarpone and whisk at low speed until creamy. Your mousse is ready.

Assembling the cake

1. Line the interior of the bowl with a layer of cling film. Try to make it fit snugly against the surface of the bowl and make sure that it flows over the edges, so you can get hold of it when you have finished.
2. Slice the sponge cake into long strips about 1.5 cm (½ inch) thick.
3. In a bowl dissolve the chocolate powder with the milk.
4. Cut the strips to fit the height of your

Ingredients for the sponge cake

225 g (8 oz) [1⅔ dip-and-sweep cups] flour
(plain white flour/unbleached all purpose flour)
8 eggs
225 g (8 oz) [1 cup] sugar
Square cake tin measuring 23 cm (9 inches)

Ingredients for the mascarpone mousse

500 g (1 lb 2 oz) [2 cups] mascarpone
300 g (10½ oz) [1½ cups] sugar
8 eggs

Extra bits

Cling film
3 tablespoons hot chocolate powder
Unsweetened cocoa powder
600 ml (1 pint) [2½ cups] milk
400 ml (14 fl oz) [1⅔ cups] whipping cream (for ladybird)
Liquorice strings
Pine nuts (for hedgehog), red food colouring (for ladybird)
Dark chocolate buttons and decorative pieces for animal faces
White and dark chocolate

bowl. The strips will vary in length as you gradually line your bowl, and you will have different size off-cuts.

5. Dip the sponge strips into the chocolaty milk and line the interior of the bowl. I suggest you just dip the surface of each strip, turn it around and dip the other side. Do not immerse the full strip in milk as it will become too moist and soft. Alternatively, you could put each strip in the bowl and use a brush to moisten it with the chocolaty milk. The idea is to get the sponge moist but not to drown it in liquid.

6. Once your bowl is completely covered with sponge cake strips dipped in chocolaty milk, place a layer of mascarpone mousse over them.

7. Repeat steps 5 and 6, alternating layers of sponge strips dipped in chocolaty milk with layers of mascarpone mousse. You finish when you reach a layer of sponge cake that is flat.

8. Choose the dish where you want your 'animal' to go. Put the dish over the bowl, against the final horizontal layer, and then turn it over.

9. Gently pull off the bowl. You should have a nice dome-shaped sponge. Remove the cling film. Depending on what animal you decide to have, the final decorations will vary.

For the **ladybird**: whip the cream and with a non-serrated knife spread a layer all over the cake. Then mix some red food colouring in the remaining cream and fill a piping bag. Distribute small blobs of red cream all over the body, as shown in the picture. Melt some plain chocolate and, with a knife, evenly spread it over the one end, to make up the face. Before it dries, place two white chocolate buttons at the top (the eyes). With the melted plain chocolate, put dots on the chocolate buttons for the pupils of the eyes and draw a line over the back of the ladybird. Use the dark chocolate buttons for its spots. You can melt some white chocolate to draw the mouth. Use some liquorice strings for the antennae.

For the **hedgehog** and the **mouse**, using a non-serrated knife spread some mascarpone mousse all over the cake. Then dust it with a layer of cocoa powder. For the hedgehog's spikes you can place pine nuts all over the body, use white chocolate for the eyes, liquorice strings for its whiskers and a large chocolate button for its nose. For the mouse, you can use two large chocolate buttons for its ears, liquorice strings for its whiskers and tail, and mini sugar balls for its eyes.

Suggestion: even though this cake was primarily designed for children, you can make it for adults too, in a simpler version. You can see my own adaptation of this cake without the decorations. I replaced the chocolaty milk for the dip with Martini, but you can use espresso coffee, for instance, and I made my tiramisu mousse in two flavours by adding some melted plain chocolate to half the mousse, following my own chocolate tiramisu recipe. It's worth remembering that you can always adapt these recipes to your own needs and tastes.

To find out about Cristina see page 64.

Dalia's Tiramisu Cups

Makes 10–12 children's cups

1 extra large egg or 2 small eggs
90 g (3 oz) [½ cup] sugar
250 g (9 oz) [1 cup] mascarpone
125 ml (4 fl oz) [½ cup] whipping cream
12 sponge fingers/ladyfingers
250 ml (9 fl oz) [1 cup] milk
1 tablespoon hot chocolate powder
Cocoa powder/chocolate bits for decoration

1. Pour the cream into a bowl, add ¾ tablespoon of sugar and whip into stiff peaks. Place the cream in the fridge.
2. Separate the egg whites from the yolks. Discard the whites.
3. Whisk the egg yolks with the sugar until you obtain a light, pale mousse.
4. Place the mascarpone in a bowl and soften it with a wooden spoon.
5. Add part of the yolk/sugar mixture to the mascarpone and gently blend with the spoon.
6. Add the rest of the mixture and blend until you obtain a smooth mousse.
7. Take the whipped cream from the fridge and incorporate it into the mixture in three stages. Each time mix the cream with slow circular movements, working from the bottom of the bowl upwards.
8. Fill a large piping bag with the mascarpone mousse.
9. In a bowl dissolve the hot chocolate powder with the milk.
10. Line up the cups next to the bowl and cut the sponge fingers to fit the bottom of the cups.
11. Dip the sponge fingers in the chocolaty milk. Let them soak enough on each side to become moist but not soggy. Divide half the sponge finger pieces between the cups, placing some at the bottom of each cup.
12. Take the piping bag and squeeze the mousse over the sponge fingers. Sprinkle with cocoa powder.
13. Place another layer of dipped sponge fingers on top of the mousse.
14. Finish with another layer of mascarpone mousse.
15. Decorate with a dusting of cocoa powder and chocolate bits.
16. Refrigerate for at least four hours before serving.

My friend Dalia Portas lives near Cagliari. She's a biologist but since she got married and started a family she hasn't pursued a scientific career. She's dedicated a lot of time and energy to her two young children, a boy and a girl, and she has passion for cooking, both savoury and sweet dishes. In 2011 Dalia decorated her first cake and realized she did a pretty good job; this took her on the path of becoming a cake designer and now she travels all over Italy and runs courses on cake design and cake modelling. Her classes are always booked up and her creations are true works of art. Her favourite sweet treat is milk chocolate.

Dalia's Tiramisu Cupcakes

Makes 12 cupcakes
Using cupcake cases measuring 5 cm (2 inches) across the base

Ingredients for the cupcakes
2 eggs
100 g (3½ oz) [½ cup] sugar
125 g (4½ oz) [½ cup] mascarpone
125 g (4½ oz) [1 dip-and-sweep cup] flour
(plain white flour/unbleached all purpose flour)
1¾ teaspoons baking powder

Ingredients for the icing
1 extra large egg or 2 small eggs
90 g (3 oz) [½ cup] sugar
250 g (9 oz) [1 cup] mascarpone
125 ml (4 fl oz) [½ cup] whipping cream
Cocoa powder
4 espresso coffees
Plain chocolate

1. Whisk the eggs with the sugar until you obtain a light, pale mousse.
2. Add the mascarpone and whisk until you get a smooth cream.
3. Sieve the flour and the baking powder into the mixture and gently stir with a wooden spoon.
4. Place the cupcake cases on the baking tray and half fill each one with the cake mixture.
5. Bake in the oven at a 180°C (350° F) [Gas Mark 4] for about 20–25 minutes, or until ready. You can check if your cupcakes are ready by inserting a thin skewer in the middle. If it comes out clean, your cupcakes are done.

***

6. Pour the cream into a bowl, add ¾ tablespoon of sugar and whip into stiff peaks. Place the cream in the fridge.
7. Separate the egg whites from the yolks. Discard the whites.
8. Whisk the egg yolks with the remaining sugar until you obtain a light, pale mousse.
9. Place the mascarpone in a bowl and soften it with a wooden spoon.
10. Add part of the yolk/sugar mixture to the mascarpone and gently blend with the spoon.
11. Add the rest of the mixture and blend until you obtain a smooth mousse.
12. Take the whipped cream from the fridge and incorporate it into the mixture in three stages. Each time mix the cream with slow circular movements, working from the bottom of the bowl upwards.
13. Fill in a large piping bag with the mascarpone mousse.
14. When the cupcakes have cooled down, gently insert a small sharp knife in the middle of the top of each cupcake and cut out a cylindrical piece of cake, about 1.5 cm (half an inch) wide. Brush the inside with some espresso coffee and then the surface of each cupcake.
15. Take the piping bag and fill the inside of each cupcake with the mascarpone mousse.
16. Once the cupcakes have been filled inside, you can use the mousse for the topping, with the same piping bag but with a larger nozzle.
17. Cover the top of each cupcake with mousse and sprinkle with cocoa powder.
18. You can also decorate the cupcakes with dark chocolate, as shown in the photo.
19. Refrigerate for four hours before serving.

To find out about Dalia see page 24.

Dalia's Tiramisu Cheesecake

The ingredients are for a baking tin 18 cm (7 inches) in diameter. Even though you're using a baking tin, this is not a baked cheesecake. Dalia recommends using a springform tin as it will be easier to remove the cheesecake later. She also advises placing a layer of baking parchment at the bottom, as it will allow you to slide the cheesecake onto a plate when it's ready to be served. Dalia used instant coffee powder, not granules. Granules don't dissolve in the biscuit crumbs, or on top of the dessert. I recommend that if you use coffee granules you place them inside a plastic bag and bash them to a powder first.

Serves 6

Ingredients for the biscuit base
100 g (3½ oz) digestive biscuits (if you use the traditional McVities, this equals 7 biscuits)
40 g (1½ oz) [3 tablespoons] butter
1 tablespoon instant coffee
1 tablespoon sugar

Ingredients for the cheese mousse
250 g (9 oz) [1 cup] mascarpone
250 ml (9 fl oz) [1 cup] whipping cream
120 g (4 oz) [⅔ cup] sugar
3 eggs
10 g gelatine leaves*

Ingredients for the topping
½ tablespoon instant coffee
½ tablespoon unsweetened cocoa powder

1. Melt the butter at low heat.
2. Place the biscuits inside a plastic bag and seal it; bash them into crumbs with a rolling pin.
3. Put the crumbled biscuits in a bowl, together with the melted butter, sugar and 1 tablespoon of coffee. Mix well.
4. Spread the mixture evenly over the bottom of the tin, with the help of a spoon. Place in the fridge.
5. Soak your gelatine leaves in cold water.
6. Separate the egg whites from the yolks. Discard the whites.
7. Take a large saucepan and boil some water, then lower the heat and let it simmer.
8. Put the yolks and sugar into a bowl and place over the simmering water (bain-marie). Quickly whisk for a few minutes until you obtain a light, pale mousse. Remove from the heat and let it cool down.
9. Switch off the heat but don't throw away the water.
10. In a separate bowl, whip the cream into stiff peaks.
11. Add the mascarpone and whisk with the cream for a couple of minutes.
12. Gently add the whisked eggs and fold into the mixture with a wooden spoon.
13. Squeeze out the excess water from the gelatine leaves and place them in a small saucepan.
14. Place the saucepan over the hot water left from before and let the gelatine melt. Don't allow it to boil.
15. Quickly add the melted gelatine to the mascarpone mousse and mix well.
16. Pour the mousse over the biscuit base and distribute evenly.
17. Refrigerate for four hours.
18. Before serving, mix ½ tablespoon instant coffee and ½ tablespoon cocoa powder and dust over the dessert.

When I tried this recipe in the UK I used Dr Oetker Leaf Gelatine (20 g packet of 12 leaves). I used 6 leaves (10 g). Always read the instructions on the packet when working with gelatine.

To find out about Dalia see page 24.

Laura's Banana Tiramisu

1. Grate the zest of the lemon into a small bowl.
2. Squeeze the lemon and place the juice into another bowl.
3. Cut 300 g (10½ oz) bananas into 1 cm (⅓ inch) slices and place them in the bowl with the lemon juice; this will prevent them from going brown.
4. Separate the egg whites from the yolks and place them in different bowls.
5. Whisk the yolks with 3 tablespoons of sugar and the lemon zest until you get a light, pale mousse.
6. Add the mascarpone to the mixture; whisk at a low speed until creamy.
7. In a separate bowl, whip the cream with the remaining sugar into stiff peaks.
8. Add the cream to the mixture and gently stir in with a wooden spoon.
9. Drain three-quarters of the bananas that were in the lemon juice. Add them to the mixture and whisk with a spoon.
10. Place the chocolate and hazelnuts in a food processor. Grind them, but not too finely, and add them to the mixture. Whisk with a spoon.
11. Beat the egg whites into firm peaks.
12. Gently fold the egg whites into the mixture with slow circular movements.
13. Cut the remaining bananas into large pieces and place them into a food liquidizer. Pour the milk over them and blend.
14. Choose 6 cups and cut the sponge fingers to fit the bottom of the cups. This tiramisu will also fit a serving dish of 31 x 21 cm (about 12 x 8½ inches). If you use a serving dish, line the bottom of the dish with the sponge fingers.
15. Pour the banana milk over the sponge fingers; cover them but do not drown them.
16. Spread the mascarpone mousse over the sponge fingers.
18. Drain the banana slices that were left in the lemon juice and use them to decorate the tiramisu. You can add some whipped cream on top, if you wish.
19. Refrigerate for four hours before serving.

Suggestions: if you don't like nuts or are allergic to them, simply omit them from this recipe. This tiramisu is delicious even without the hazelnuts.

Serves 6

500 g bananas (1 lb 2 oz) (weight of fruit without the skins)
3 eggs
5 tablespoons sugar
200 ml (7 fl oz) [¾ cup] whipping cream
200 ml (7 fl oz) [¾ cup] milk
250 g (9 oz) [1 cup] mascarpone
100g (3½ oz) block of plain chocolate
100 g (3½ oz) [¾ cup] shelled whole hazelnuts
1 organic lemon
12–15 sponge fingers/ladyfingers

My friend Laura Puddu is studying Political Sciences at the University of Cagliari. She loves baking and making desserts, and she's very good at it; that's why I had to include her delicious Banana Tiramisu in my book. Laura has multiple interests: she's into swimming and listening to music, and she's a keen reader. She also has a passion for photography; she will take a shot of anything that catches her curiosity, whether it's people or scenery. Laura loves writing; she dreams of becoming a journalist one day, and of travelling the world. Her biggest dream is to become a National Geographic reporter. Her favourite dessert is ice cream.

Rita's Pineapple Tiramisu

Serves 6

9 pineapple rings
3 eggs
5 tablespoons sugar
200 ml (7 fl oz) [¾ cup] whipping cream
250 g (9 oz) [1 cup] mascarpone
1 tablespoon of rum
12–15 sponge fingers/ladyfingers
200 ml (7 fl oz) [¾ cup] pineapple juice

This tiramisu is made with tinned pineapples. It's very refreshing and it's ideal if you fancy an exotic dessert but can't get hold of the fresh fruit.

1. Separate the egg whites from the yolks and place them in different bowls.
2. Whisk the yolks with 3 tablespoons of sugar until you get a light, pale mousse.
3. Add the mascarpone and rum to the mixture, whisk at a low speed until creamy.
4. In a separate bowl, whip the cream with the remaining sugar into stiff peaks.
5. Add the cream to the mixture and gently stir with a wooden spoon.
6. Take 3 pineapple rings and cut them into small pieces. Add them to the mascarpone mousse and mix.
7. Beat the egg whites into firm peaks.
8. Gently fold the egg whites into the mixture with slow circular movements.
9. Choose 6 cups and place the sponge fingers at the bottom of the cups. This tiramisu will also fit a serving dish of 30 x 22 cm (12 x 8½ inches). If you use a serving dish, line the bottom of the dish with the sponge fingers.
10. Pour the pineapple juice over the sponge fingers; let them soak enough to become moist, but they must not drown.
11. Spread the mousse over the sponge fingers.
12. Place the remaining pineapple rings on top of the mascarpone mousse.
13. You can decorate your tiramisu with some whipped cream, if you wish.
14. Refrigerate for four hours before serving.

Suggestions: fresh fruit always tastes better than tinned fruit. If you can get hold of a sweet fresh pineapple, this dessert will be a real treat.

Rita Puddu is my oldest friend. She would deserve a special chapter in this book, because it's thanks to her that I got to taste my first ever tiramisu. We were only teenagers at the time and she told me about this wonderful dessert that her brother had made (he was a chef) which I had to try, but she wouldn't tell me what was in it, as she was afraid I'd run away at the thought of raw eggs. I loved it. I even had seconds. And then she told me. I didn't know whether to kill her or not. But I forgave her and I've had tiramisu hundreds of times since. Rita lives in Cagliari with her husband. She is a wonderful cook and I have learnt so many recipes from her; in fact she has contributed a few pasta sauce recipes to my other book. She throws the most amazing dinner parties. When you're lucky enough to be invited to her home, whether it's just for a quick spaghettata or for a more formal occasion, you always feel well looked after; it's Sardinian hospitality at its best. Her favourite dessert is traditional tiramisu.

Rita's Orange Tiramisu

Serves 6

3 eggs
5 tablespoons sugar
2 organic oranges
200 ml (7 fl oz) [¾ cup] whipping cream
250 g (9 oz) [1 cup] mascarpone
2 tablespoons of Cointreau
200 ml (7 fl oz) [¾ cup] milk
12 sponge fingers/ladyfingers
100g (3½ oz) block of plain chocolate

1. Wash both oranges.
2. Grate the zest of one of the oranges onto a small bowl.
3. With the second orange you need to prepare glazed orange peel, which will go into the mascarpone mousse. Cut the top and the bottom off and peel the orange into 6-8 vertical segments. Place the peel in a small saucepan, cover with cold water and boil for one minute. Strain the peel. Repeat this process two more times.
4. Put the peel back in the saucepan, and add one cup of water and one cup of sugar. It doesn't matter what size the cup is, as long as the volume is the same. I used a 250 ml (9 fl oz) cup. Place the saucepan over a low heat and let it simmer.
5. At some point, after the water has evaporated, the sugar will start to crystallize. Before it becomes hard, remove the orange peel and place on greaseproof paper. Let it cool down.
6. Separate the egg whites from the yolks and place them in different bowls.
7. Whisk the yolks with 3 tablespoons of sugar until you get a light, pale mousse.
8. Add the mascarpone, 1 tablespoon of Cointreau and orange zest to the mixture; whisk at a low speed until creamy.
9. In a separate bowl, whip the cream and the rest of the sugar into stiff peaks.
10. Add the cream to the mixture and gently stir with a wooden spoon.
11. Cut the glazed orange peel in small pieces and add to the mixture.
12. Beat the egg whites into firm peaks.
13. Gently fold the egg whites into the mixture with slow circular movements.
14. Pour the milk into a bowl and add 1 tablespoon of Cointreau to the milk.
15. Choose 6 cups and line them up next to the bowl.
16. Dip the sponge fingers into the milk; let them soak enough to become moist but not soggy. Spread them over the bottoms of all 6 cups.
17. Grate some chocolate over the sponge fingers.
18. Place a thick layer of mascarpone mousse over the biscuits.
19. Sprinkle some grated chocolate over the mousse.
20. Peel each orange segment, so that only the flesh is showing. Discard the pips. Cut the segments into small pieces and set aside. Place the desserts and the fruit in the fridge for four hours before serving.
21. When you're about to serve the tiramisu, place the orange pieces on top of the mascarpone mousse. Decorate with whipped cream, if you wish.

Suggestions: this tiramisu is delicious and has a very delicate flavour. I found that the most challenging part was getting the glazed orange peel right. I tried several times, and if you're new to the process, you may want to experiment with this bit first. It would be a good idea to glaze your orange peel the night before you make your dessert, for instance, just in case. Before I finally got it right, my efforts resulted in orange peel that was as hard as a rock. On one occasion the water in my saucepan evaporated completely and I found myself with an unbreakable layer of sugar and the peel buried underneath it. I ended up yelling at my friend Rita over the phone. In a typical Italian way of communicating she just yelled back and said "Just go and buy some from the shop!"

To find out about Rita, see page 32.

Manuela's Tiramisu Brownie

This brownie is made up of two parts. The base is a classic chocolate brownie, with a hint of coffee. This is topped by a second layer made with mascarpone and cream cheese which gets baked together with the brownie, giving it the consistency on top of a baked cheesecake. The result is really yummy. Manuela recommends that you keep some of the mascarpone mousse aside and serve it with your brownie, ideally dusted with a little cocoa powder, as shown in the picture.

Making the brownie

1. Line your tin with baking parchment.
2. Cut the chocolate into pieces and put them in a small saucepan with the butter.
3. Place the saucepan over simmering water (bain-marie), and let the chocolate and butter melt.
4. When the chocolate and butter are melted, turn off the heat and remove the saucepan from the water. Add the coffee and stir.
5. In a separate bowl mix the flour and the sugar.
6. Add the melted coffee/butter/chocolate to the flour and sugar and stir together well.
7. In a separate bowl whisk the eggs until light and frothy.
8. Add the eggs to the mixture and combine until you have a smooth consistency.
9. Set a small quantity (about one fifth) of the mixture aside and pour the rest into the cake tin. Spread evenly.

Making the baked cheesecake layer

1. Separate the egg whites from the yolks and place them in different bowls.
2. Whisk the yolks with the sugar until you get a light, pale mousse.
3. Add the mascarpone and cream cheese, and mix until you obtain a smooth mixture.

Serves 8–10
For a square 23 cm (9 inch) baking tin

Ingredients for the brownie
3 100g (3 ½ oz) blocks of plain chocolate
225 g (8 oz) [2 sticks] butter
200 g (7 oz) [1 cup] sugar
4 whole eggs plus 2 egg whites
150 g (5 oz) [1 dip-and-sweep cup] flour
(plain white flour/unbleached all purpose flour)
4 espresso coffees (about 200 ml) (7 fl oz) [¾ cup] – sweetened to taste

My friend Manuela Paric' lives in Piacenza with her young daughter and several pets, which include chubby cats, well-nourished dogs and mutant fish. I have great admiration for her, because she's a single mum who works very hard in advertising, she's extremely talented and she manages to balance her demanding job with being a great mum. Food is a real passion for her; she started making a mess of the cooker as young as five, thanks to her dad, and at the age of 15 she had managed to prepare a Christmas meal for the whole family, and we're talking of an Italian Christmas meal! Her top dish is gnocchi della nonna (grandma's gnocchi).
Manuela also writes noir fiction, and her books are real page turners.
Her favourite dessert is ice cream.

Ingredients for the baked cheesecake layer

350 g (12½ oz) [1⅓ cups] mascarpone
250 g (9 oz) [1 cup] Philadelphia cream cheese
75 g (2½ oz) [⅓ cup] sugar
2 whole eggs plus 2 egg yolks

(You will need a total of 8 eggs: when you separate the eggs for the brownie to obtain the 2 whites, just make sure you set aside the 2 yolks to use for the baked cheesecake layer.)

4. Beat the egg whites until they form stiff peaks.
5. With a wooden spoon, fold the egg whites into the cheese mousse, with slow movements, working from the bottom of the bowl upwards.
6. Your cheese mousse is ready to be spread over the chocolate brownie part. At this point you have to decide whether you want to set some aside to be served as a cream to go with your brownie later, or whether you want to bake the whole lot. If you want to set some aside, I recommend you place about a quarter of the mousse in a jug and refrigerate it straight away.
7. Pour the cheese mousse over the chocolate mixture in the tin and spread evenly.
8. Take the small quantity of chocolate mixture left from before and decorate the top of your cheese mousse with it. It may be helpful to use a piping bag or a spoon.
9. Bake in the oven at 180°C (350° F) [Gas Mark 4] for 40–45 minutes. Unlike conventional cakes, for this one, when you test it with a skewer, you shouldn't expect it to come out clean. The cheesecake should still be a little soft in the middle. If the sides of the cake are starting to pull away from the tin, and the top looks golden and it shows some cracks, it's likely to be done.
10. When the cake is ready, remove it from the oven, let it cool down and then place it in the fridge (unless you eat it straight away!).

Suggestions: Normally chocolate brownies wouldn't need to be kept in the fridge, but this one, because it has a cheesecake part to it, needs to be refrigerated. The downside to this is that the cold can make the brownie part go a little hard. One way around this is to take the dessert out of the fridge 10–15 minutes before you serve it; that seems to do the trick.

Ferruccio's Tiramisu Cake

Ferruccio made this tiramisu cake for his son's second birthday, hence the unusual decorations. The cake is made up of two sponge cakes, one on top of the other, with a layer of chocolate mascarpone mousse in the middle. Each sponge is dipped in chocolate milk, but if you make this cake for adults, you can use espresso coffee instead. The cake has a simple buttercream icing and is dusted with cocoa powder on top.

Making the sponge cakes

1. Separate the egg whites from the yolks and place them in different bowls.
2. Add the sugar to the yolks and whisk for several minutes until light and fluffy.
3. Sieve the flour and baking powder into the bowl and mix with a wooden spoon.
4. Add a pinch of salt to the egg whites and beat them into stiff peaks.
5. Fold the egg whites into the yolk mixture with gentle circular movements, working from the bottom of the bowl upwards.
6. Grease the cake tin and dust with flour.
7. Pour the mixture into the cake tin and bake at 180°C (350° F) [Gas Mark 4] for 25–30 minutes or until ready. You can check if your cake is ready by inserting a thin skewer in the middle. If it comes out clean, your cake is done.
8. Repeat the above for the second sponge cake.

Making the chocolate mousse filling

1. Cut the chocolate into pieces and place them in a small saucepan.
2. Place the small saucepan with the chocolate over a pan of simmering water (bain-marie) and let the chocolate melt.
3. When the chocolate is melted, switch off the heat, and leave the pan over the hot water.
4. Separate the egg whites from the yolks and place them in different bowls.

Serves 10-12

Ingredients for one sponge cake

As you're making two of these cakes, you will need to double the quantities.

(cake tin measuring 26 cm
10½ inches in diameter)
6 eggs
180 g (6½ oz) [¾ cup] sugar
180 g (6½ oz) [1¼ dip-and-sweep cups] flour
(plain white flour/unbleached all purpose flour)
2 teaspoons baking powder

Ferruccio Munzittu is my youngest brother and he lives near Treviso with his wife and young son. He likes to experiment with new things, hence the slightly whacky decorations on this cake. As a little boy he was a bit of a rascal and very good at getting into trouble. I, as the big sister, was charged with the difficult task of keeping him out of mischief. As an adult, he has become more sensible (we hope) and he now works in an office for a transport logistics company. That hasn't dented his sense of humour and, given the chance, he will always do something funny and make you laugh. In his spare time Ferruccio likes to play with his young son, read as many books as possible and learn new IT skills (he created my author website). He also loves to go for walks and take photos of the beautiful Veneto scenery. His favourite dessert is crème caramel.

Ingredients for chocolate mascarpone cream filling

100g (3½ oz) block of plain chocolate
250 g (9 oz) [1 cup] mascarpone
150 g (5 oz) [¾ cup] sugar
4 eggs

Ingredients for buttercream icing and other bits

250 g (9 oz) [1 cup] unsalted butter
500 g (1 lb 2 oz) [2½ cups] sugar
300 ml (½ pint) [1¼ cups] milk
2 tablespoons hot chocolate powder
3 tablespoons unsweetened cocoa powder
Chocolate Swiss rolls/fingers to decorate cake

5. Whisk the yolks with the sugar until you get a light, pale mousse.
6. Add the mascarpone and whisk at a low speed until creamy.
7. Add the melted chocolate and mix.
8. Beat the egg whites into firm peaks.
9. Fold in half (only half) of the egg whites into the mixture. Use a wooden spoon and mix with gentle circular movements. If the chocolate mousse is too dense, add a little extra egg white to make it lighter.
10. Place the mousse in the fridge.

Making the icing

1. Place the softened butter in a bowl and beat it with a spoon until creamy.
2. Sift the sugar on top of it and mix the ingredients until smooth.
3. The buttercream is ready to be spread over the cake.

Putting it all together

1. Pour the milk into a bowl and add the hot chocolate powder. Mix well. If you're making this cake for adults, you can replace the chocolaty milk with espresso coffee.
2. Brush one side of each sponge cake with the chocolaty milk, the sides that are facing upwards. The sponge must be moist but not soaked.
3. Spread the chocolate mascarpone mousse all over one sponge cake.
4. With a gentle but firm movement, take the other sponge cake and flip it on top of the one with the mascarpone mousse. The side that was soaked in chocolaty milk has to be in contact with the mousse. The chocolate mascarpone is now sandwiched between two sponge cakes.
5. Spread a layer of buttercream all over the cake. The quantities are very generous and you may have some icing left over.
6. With a fine sieve, dust the cocoa powder on top of the cake.
7. The final decorations are up to you. On this cake Ferruccio used some chocolate Swiss rolls and chocolate fingers, his son's favourites.

Suggestions: considering the lengthy process, if you're making this cake for a special occasion and don't have much time, you can split the preparations over three days. For instance, you could bake the sponge cakes on day 1, let them cool down and wrap them in cling film so that they stay moist. On day 2 you could prepare the mascarpone mousse and refrigerate it. On day 3, you can assemble the cake and decorate it.

Mariangela's Strawberry Tiramisu

Serves 6

4 eggs
150 g (5 oz) [¾ cup] sugar
200 g (7 oz) pack of sponge fingers/ladyfingers
250 g (9 oz) [1 cup] mascarpone
2 tablespoons of Cointreau
300 ml (½ pint) [1¼ cups] tropical fruit juice
250 g (9 oz) fresh strawberries

1. Wash the strawberries and cut them into slices
2. Separate the egg whites from the yolks and place them in different bowls.
3. Whisk the yolks with the sugar until you get a light, pale mousse.
4. Add the mascarpone and whisk at a low speed until creamy.
5. Beat the egg whites into firm peaks.
6. Gently fold the egg whites into the mixture with slow circular movements.
7. Pour the fruit juice into a bowl and add the Cointreau. Stir.
8. Choose your serving dish. The one in the picture is 20 x 20 cm (8 x 8 inches).
9. Dip the sponge fingers into the juice; they must become moist but not soggy.
10. Place half of them in a layer over the bottom of your dish.
11. Spread a layer of mascarpone mousse over the sponge fingers.
12. Distribute half the strawberries over the mousse.
13. Place another layer of sponge fingers dipped into the fruit juice.
14. Add another layer of mascarpone mousse.
15. Decorate the dessert with the remaining strawberries.

Suggestions: children love strawberries. If you want to serve this tiramisu to children too, just omit the Cointreau from the list of ingredients.

*Mariangela Panu is my sister-in-law. She's married to my brother Ferruccio and they live near Treviso with their little boy, my gorgeous nephew. She made this yummy tiramisu for St Valentine's Day. Mariangela works in quality control for a furniture retailer. She has great taste in décor and her home is always very elegant and stylish, despite the presence of an active toddler who has lots of toys! Mariangela has a passion for good food; in fact she has prepared some lovely pasta sauce recipes for my other book. She loves reading and will grab a book whenever she gets the chance. She belongs to a choir: she has an angelic voice and it's a real pleasure to hear her sing.
Her favourite dessert is crème brûlée.*

Rita's Tiramisu Pancakes

Serves 6

Ingredients for the mascarpone mousse
250 g (9 oz) [1 cup] mascarpone
3 eggs
5 tablespoons sugar
1 espresso coffee
cocoa powder

Ingredients for the pancakes
150 g (5 oz) [1 dip-and-sweep cup] flour
(plain white flour/unbleached all purpose flour)
2 tablespoons of sugar
200 ml (7 fl oz) [¾ cup] milk
1 egg
½ teaspoon unsalted butter

Making the mascarpone mousse
1. Separate the egg whites from the yolks and place them in different bowls.
2. Whisk the yolks with the sugar until you get a light, pale mousse.
3. Add the mascarpone and whisk at a low speed until creamy.
4. Beat the egg whites into firm peaks.
5. Gently fold the egg whites into the mixture with slow circular movements.
6. Add the espresso coffee and mix.
7. Refrigerate for at least two hours.

Making the pancakes
1. Whisk the egg with the milk and the softened butter in a bowl.
2. Add the flour and the sugar and whisk until you get a smooth batter.
3. Take a frying pan of 15 cm (6 inches) diameter, and wipe the inside with a piece of kitchen roll dipped in oil. Place the pan over a medium heat for a minute.
4. Pour a ladle of batter into the pan and swirl it around to distribute it evenly.
5. Cook the pancake until you notice it starts to come loose and the underside is golden-brown; then it's time to turn it over.
6. Toss the pancake and cook the other side.
7. Repeat for each pancake. You may want to grease the pan with the kitchen paper dipped in oil every two pancakes.
8. Take the mascarpone mousse from the fridge and place a couple of spoonfuls on top of each pancake. Fold the pancake. Dust with cocoa powder. Decorate with chocolate sticks or use whatever decoration you like.

Suggestions: you can prepare the mascarpone mousse the day before and keep it in the fridge ready for when you make the pancakes. If you're making these for adults, you can also add one small glass of Marsala wine to the mousse.

*My friend Rita Dessì lives in Cagliari with her husband. She's now retired after having worked for forty-three years. She's managed to raise four children while working full-time. I've always been impressed at how organized she is and what a great family she has. Despite the fact that she's no longer working, she manages to keep busy, packing her days with fun activities with her grandchildren. Rita has a passion for cooking and she's currently sharing it with her 9- and 10-year-old grandchildren. She loves going for walks and she takes a stroll in the city every day, either in the parks or along Cagliari's Poetto beach. Rita also loves to travel and she often goes away for long weekends, visiting other Italian cities in order to discover the sights, find new piazzas and sample the local cuisine. Some evenings you might also bump into her at the cinema or at the opera, in the Sardinian capital.
Her favourite dessert is ice cream.*

Martina's Chocolate Tiramisu

Serves 6–8

100g (3½ oz) block of plain chocolate
250 g (9 oz) [1 cup] mascarpone
150 g (5 oz) [¾ cup] sugar
4 eggs
300 g sponge fingers/ladyfingers* - they usually come in 200 g (7 oz) packs
300 ml (½ pint) [1¼ cups] Martini (white or red)
Unsweetened cocoa powder

*These quantities of sponge fingers are for a dessert served in a dish measuring 19 x 26 cm (7½ x 10½ inches). If you use single cups, you may need less sponge fingers.

1. Cut the chocolate into pieces and put it in a small saucepan.
2. Place the saucepan with the chocolate over simmering water (bain-marie), and let the chocolate melt.
3. When the chocolate is melted, turn off the heat, and leave the pan over the hot water.
4. Separate the egg whites from the yolks and place them in different bowls.
5. Whisk the yolks with the sugar until you get a light, pale mousse.
6. Add the mascarpone and whisk at a low speed until creamy.
7. Beat the egg whites into firm peaks.
8. Empty half of the egg yolk mixture into a bowl, add the melted chocolate, and mix.
9. Fold in half (only half) of the egg whites into the chocolate mousse. Use a wooden spoon and mix with gentle circular movements until you get a smooth cream. If the chocolate mousse is too dense, add a little extra egg white to make it lighter.
10. Choose your serving dish. It could either be 6 large cups or a ceramic/glass dish.
11. Pour the Martini into a bowl; add 150 ml (¼ pint) water. Mix.
12. Dip the sponge fingers into the Martini; they must become moist but not soggy. Place half of them at the bottom of the cups or in a layer over the bottom of your dish.
13. Spread the chocolate mousse on top of the sponge fingers.
14. Repeat another layer of sponge fingers dipped in Martini.
15. Spread the mascarpone mousse over the second layer of sponge fingers.
16. Refrigerate for at least four hours.
17. Dust with cocoa powder before serving.

Martina Munzittu lives in Cambridgeshire, with her husband and young daughter. She loves to cook, but more than that, she loves to eat, especially cakes and desserts, which is a problem when you're trying to keep in shape. One of Martina's passions is writing fiction. She has published three books so far, in both English and Italian; she would like to write a few more novels as there are many stories in her heart that are just waiting to be told. There's also one more thing that she adores and that is playing the electric guitar, although at the moment Fenderina, (that is the name of her guitar) doesn't get much attention. Martina used to play hard rock/heavy metal with some friends from work, some time ago. She's hoping one day to form an all-girl rock band, and she's already got the name for it: The Heavy-Petal Band. Now she just needs to find the girls... Her favourite dessert is ice cream.

Martina's Lemon Curd Tiramisu

Serves 6

250 g (9oz) [1 cup] mascarpone
3 tablespoons sugar
4 eggs
10 shortbread biscuits
300 g (10½ oz) [1 cup] lemon curd

1. Separate the egg whites from the yolks and place them in different bowls.
2. Whisk the yolks with the sugar until you get a light, pale mousse.
3. Add the mascarpone and whisk at a low speed until creamy.
4. Beat the egg whites into stiff peaks.
5. Fold in half (only half) of the egg whites into the mousse. Use a wooden spoon and mix with gentle circular movements until you get a smooth cream.
6. Pour the lemon curd into a small bowl; stir it with a spoon until it's soft and creamy.
7. Pour half of the mascarpone mousse into another bowl and add three-quarters of the lemon curd. Mix well but gently, as you don't want to make the egg whites runny again.
8. You now have two types of mascarpone mousse: a lemony one and a normal one.
9. Place your biscuits inside a plastic bag, seal it and bash them into crumbs with a rolling pin.
10. Choose 6 cups or glasses and place a layer of normal mascarpone mousse at the bottom of each one.
11. Add a layer of crumbled biscuits over the mousse.
12. Place a layer of lemony mousse over the biscuits.
13. Add another layer of biscuits over the lemony mousse.
14. Repeat with another layer of normal mousse.
15. You can carry on with other layers as you wish.
16. Add a swirl of lemon curd on top of the final layer of mascarpone mousse.
17. Refrigerate for four hours before serving.

Note: Depending on the size of your cups/glasses, you may be able to get more than six portions from this dessert.

To find out about Martina, see page 46.

Maria Grazia's Baileys Tiramisu

Serves 4

4 eggs
250 g (9 oz) [1 cup] mascarpone
150 g (5 oz) [¾ cup] sugar
250 ml (9 fl oz) [1 cup] Baileys
16 sponge fingers/ladyfingers
50 g (2 oz) plain chocolate

1. Separate the egg whites from the yolks. Discard the whites.
2. Whisk the yolks with the sugar until you get a light, pale mousse.
3. Add the mascarpone and whisk at a low speed until creamy.
4. Add half the amount of Baileys to the mousse and whisk.
5. Place the rest of the Baileys in a bowl and add 125 ml (4 fl oz) [½ cup] of water. Stir.
6. Choose 4 whisky glasses and place a layer of mascarpone mousse at the bottom of each glass.
7. Sprinkle some grated chocolate on top of the mousse.
8. Dip your sponge fingers in the diluted Baileys. They must become moist but not soggy. Place them in a layer on top of the mousse.
9. Spread another layer of mousse over the sponge fingers.
10. Repeat with another layer of sponge fingers dipped in Baileys.
11. Sprinkle some grated chocolate over the sponge fingers.
12. Finish with a layer of mascarpone mousse and the rest of the grated chocolate on top.
13. Refrigerate for four hours before serving.

My sister Maria Grazia Munzittu loves Baileys, so she thought of combining her favourite drink with her favourite dessert. She lives in Nanyuki, Kenya, and runs a charity which cares for fifty children, mostly orphans, affected by AIDS and HIV. She doesn't have any children herself and she considers these youngsters as her own family; with them she shares dreams and aspirations for a bright and healthier future.

Maria Grazia loves Africa and at every opportunity she tries to discover more about this country, travelling to different parts and going on safari trips. But on a daily basis, when she has the time, she likes to go for a walk and watch the huge sky and surrounding nature. She loves reading poetry, meditation and prayer.

Her favourite dessert is classic tiramisu.

Martina's Tiramisu Ice Cream

The beauty of this dessert is that you don't need an ice cream machine. You can make it at home with a bowl of ice and cold water. You may have noticed that ice cream appears several times in this book as people's favourite dessert. It happens to be mine too. Some people may think that ice cream is not much of a treat. To those people I say, if you ever travel to Italy try gelato made in a gelateria artigianale. Then you will know what Italians mean when they say that there is no better dessert. But in the meantime, try making this at home. It still reminds me of the good flavours of Italy.

1. Grate the chocolate. You can place it in a food processor or grate it by hand. Set aside.
2. Separate the egg whites from the yolks. Discard the whites and place the yolks in a bowl.
3. Add the sugar to the yolks and place the bowl over simmering water (bain-marie). Quickly whisk for a few minutes, add the milk and whisk until the liquid reduces. Remove the bowl and turn off the heat.
4. Take a very large bowl and fill it two-thirds full with ice cubes, cold water and some salt.
5. Place the bowl with the egg yolk mixture in the ice bath. Add the mascarpone and whisk at a low speed until creamy.
6. Add the cream and whisk for 2–3 minutes.
7. Add the grated chocolate and whisk at low speed for 2 minutes.
8. Choose your container. Remove the mousse from the ice bath and pour it into the container.
9. Freeze overnight or for at least 12 hours.
10. Remove the ice cream from the freezer 5–10 minutes before serving, as it tends to be harder than normal ice cream.
11. You can serve the ice cream as it is, or you can dip some sponge fingers in espresso coffee (as shown in the picture) and place the ice cream balls on top.

Suggestions: here is an alternative to the simple ice cream. Before you freeze the mousse, you can dip the sponge fingers in coffee, place a layer of half the sponge fingers on the bottom of your container and pour half the ice cream over them. Then repeat with another layer of sponge fingers and finish with a layer of ice cream. You could then freeze the dessert as it is, and serve it a tiramisu gelato.

To find out about Martina, see page 46.

Serves 6

250 g (9 oz) [1 cup] mascarpone
250 g (9 fl oz) [1 cup] double cream
5 tablespoons sugar
2 eggs
1 tablespoon milk
100 g (3½ oz) block of plain chocolate
200 g (7 oz) sponge fingers/ladyfingers
250 ml (9 fl oz) [1 cup] espresso coffee
Plenty of ice

Maria Antonietta's Gluten-Free Tiramisu

Maria Antonietta has a sister who suffers with coeliac disease; hence she's not allowed any gluten in her diet. In Italy you can buy gluten-free sponge fingers in specialist shops and chemists, but Maria Antonietta is a keen baker and she likes to prepare her own sponge cake for the tiramisu.

Serves 6

Ingredients for the gluten-free sponge cake
4 eggs
150 g (5 oz) [¾ cup] sugar
75 g (2½ oz) [½ dip-and-sweep cup] gluten-free flour
75 g (2½ oz) [½ dip-and-sweep cup] potato flour
2 teaspoons baking powder

Ingredients for the mascarpone mousse and for dipping
250 g (9 oz) [1 cup] mascarpone
3 eggs
6 tablespoons sugar
125 ml (4 fl oz) [½ cup] whipping cream
300 ml (½ pint) [1¼ cups] espresso coffee
Unsweetened cocoa powder

Making the sponge cake
1. Separate the egg whites from the yolks and place them in different bowls.
2. Add the sugar to the yolks and whisk for several minutes until light and fluffy.
3. Sieve both types of flour and the baking powder into the bowl and mix with a wooden spoon.
4. Add a pinch of salt to the egg whites and beat them into stiff peaks.
5. Fold the egg whites into the mixture with gentle circular movements, working from the bottom of the bowl upwards.
6. Grease the cake tin and dust with gluten-free flour.
7. Pour the mixture into the cake tin and bake at 180°C (350° F) [Gas Mark 4] for 20-25 minutes or until ready. You can check if your cake is ready by inserting a thin skewer in the middle. If it comes out clean, your cake is done.

Making the mascarpone mousse
1. Separate the egg whites from the yolks and place them in different bowls. Discard one egg white; use only two.
2. Whisk the yolks with the sugar until you get a light, pale mousse.
3. Add the mascarpone to the mixture and whisk at a low speed until creamy.
4. In a separate bowl, whip the cream into stiff peaks.
5. Add the cream to the mixture and gently stir with a wooden spoon.
6. Beat the egg whites into firm peaks.
7. Gently fold the egg whites into the mixture with slow circular movements.

My cousin Maria Antonietta Munzittu is one of four cousins who lived next door to our family home in Sardinia. We often played together, either at our house or at hers, and at family get-togethers we would let the grown-ups talk or eat while we would just have fun. She's now a very busy mum of three, and with her partner runs a stall selling shoes at local markets. Maria Antonietta is a great cook. She's prepared a fantastic seafood risotto for my risotto recipe book, and she always likes to experiment in the kitchen, baking some wonderful cakes and pastries. She loves listening to music; Latin American is her favourite. The dessert of her choice is the classic tiramisu.

Putting it all together

1. Once the sponge cake has cooled down, cut it in strips about 1½ cm (½ inch) wide, the thickness of a sponge finger. You can adjust the length of the strips to fit the size of your serving dish.
   For this dessert Maria Antonietta used a dish measuring 20 x 25 cm (8 x 10 inches).
2. Line the bottom of your dish with half of the strips of sponge cake.
3. Pour some coffee over the strips of cake, enough for them to become moist but not soggy.
4. Spread half of the mascarpone mousse over the strips of cake.
5. Place the remaining coffee in a bowl and dip the other half of the cake strips in it, one at a time. Unlike sponge fingers, this cake absorbs the liquid very quickly, so you have to dip it in and out, otherwise it will disintegrate in the bowl.
6. Place the strips of sponge cake dipped in coffee over the mascarpone mousse, forming a second layer.
7. Spread the remaining mascarpone mousse over the cake strips.
8. Dust with cocoa powder.
9. Refrigerate for four hours before serving.

Suggestions: potato flour gives this cake a softer texture, but it's not easy to find it in shops. If you struggle to get hold of it, you can replace it with corn flour. Alternatively you can bake this cake just with gluten-free flour.

Tiziana's Peach Tiramisu

Serves 6

12 half peaches in syrup
250 g (9 oz) [1 cup] mascarpone
300 ml (½ pint) [1¼ cups] double cream
4 tablespoons sugar
3 eggs
9 shortbread biscuits

1. Drain the peaches and set the syrup aside.
2. Cut the peaches into slices.
3. Separate the egg whites from the yolks. Discard the whites.
4. Whisk the yolks with the sugar until you get a light, pale mousse.
5. Add the mascarpone and whisk at a low speed until creamy.
6. Add the cream and 3 tablespoons of the peach syrup and whisk for a couple of minutes.
7. Place the biscuits inside a plastic bag, seal it and bash them into crumbs with a rolling pin.
8. Choose 6 cups or glasses and place a layer of crumbled biscuits at the bottom of each cup.
9. Place a layer of mousse on top of the biscuits.
10. Lay half the peach slices over the mousse.
11. Finish with another layer of mascarpone mousse.
12. Decorate with the remaining peach slices.

Note: these are generous portions. Depending on the size of your cups, and how thickly you cut your peaches, you may be able to have more than two layers of mascarpone mousse, or prepare more than six cups.

Suggestions: if you can find fresh sweet peaches, this dessert will taste even better. Unfortunately it's difficult to find great tasting fruit that is not grown locally. Somehow, when peaches are transported from a long distance, they get spoilt. I find that tinned peaches are a reasonable compromise, in the absence of a good fresh alternative.

Tiziana Munzittu is my niece; she's the daughter of my second brother, Mariano. She lives in Uta, not far from Cagliari. She works as an administrative assistant in a busy office, but during her spare time she likes to keep fit in the gym or play basketball and she enjoys going out with her friends. Tiziana loves to read serious books, the ones that tell you stories about hardship and people who struggle in different parts of the world, so no real escapism there. However, except for winter, she reads her books mostly on the beach, while listening to the sound of the waves and the cries of seagulls. She would love to travel the world and take lots of photos of all the countries she visits, so that one day, when she moves into her own place, she can hang all those pictures on her walls. Her favourite dessert is fruit of the forest cheesecake.

Sofia's Rainbow Tiramisu

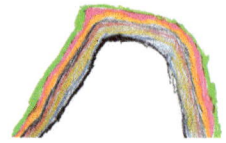

Makes 8 children cups

4 eggs
250 g (9 oz) [1 cup] mascarpone
150 g (5 oz) [¾ cup] sugar
16 sponge fingers/ladyfingers
2 tablespoons hot chocolate powder
300ml (½ pint) [1¼ cups] milk
Cocoa powder
1 pack of M&M chocolate buttons

My four-year-old daughter Sofia has shown a lot of interest in my tiramisu making. She's been wanting to test the recipes with me and she has always been keen to lick the spoon at the end, especially when it is chocolaty. Children are curious and often want to get involved in the kitchen and I believe that they should be encouraged, considering they will be the cooks of tomorrow. Sofia has been heavily involved in making this tiramisu: she has helped to whisk the eggs with the sugar, dip the biscuits in the milk, dust the mousse with cocoa powder and, most important of all, place the chocolate buttons on top of the dessert. She also picked the name. Perhaps you could try and have some fun making this tiramisu with your child.

1. Separate the egg whites from the yolks and place them in different bowls.
2. Whisk the egg yolks with the sugar until you obtain a light, pale mousse.
3. Add the mascarpone to the mixture and whisk at a low speed.
4. Beat the egg whites into stiff peaks.
5. Gently fold the egg whites into the mixture with slow circular movements.
6. Fill a large piping bag with the mousse.
7. In a bowl dissolve the hot chocolate powder with the milk.
8. Line up the cups next to the bowl and cut the sponge fingers to fit the bottoms of the cups.
9. Dip the sponge fingers in the chocolaty milk. Let them soak enough on each side to become moist but not soggy. Place the sponge fingers at the bottom of each cup.
10. Take the piping bag and squeeze half the mousse over the sponge fingers. Dust with cocoa powder.
11. Place another layer of dipped sponge fingers on top of the mousse.
12. Finish with another layer of mascarpone mousse.
13. Dust with cocoa powder.
14. Decorate with chocolate buttons.
15. Refrigerate for at least four hours before serving.

Sofia Rossiter lives with her mum and dad in Cambridgeshire. She loves to draw, to play with her doll's house and to jump on her trampoline. Sofia has great fun with her toys: a multitude of characters who wouldn't normally hang around with each other, and yet they end up being thrown together in unusual situations which could range from a relaxed picnic in a park to struggling against giant waves in a pirate ship.
Sofia has many dreams and aspirations, which seem to vary on a daily basis; they include wanting to be a princess, a super-hero, a fairy and a mermaid. Her favourite dessert is ice cream.

Mamma's Panettone Tiramisu

Serves 4

250 g (9 oz) [1 cup] mascarpone
150 g (5 oz) [¾ cup] sugar
3 eggs
3 organic oranges
450 g (1 lb) panettone
plain chocolate

It's typical, after the Christmas season, to have lots of unopened boxes of panettone lying around in an Italian home. By the time January comes, you've had enough of that cake and just want to try something different. My mum has come up with the idea of a panettone tiramisu, which is brilliant because when you do savour this dessert, you don't even think about panettone and yet those Christmassy flavours just sneak in and give it a nice magic touch. You have to try it, to see what I mean.

1. Turn the oven on at 160°C (320° F) [Gas Mark 3].
2. Cut the panettone into slices about 1½ cm (½ inch) thick.
3. If you serve this tiramisu in glasses/cups, as shown in the picture, cut the slices of panettone in circles with a biscuit cutter, to fit the size of your cups. You will need three circles per cup; that is a total of 12 panettone circles.
4. Place the panettone circles on a baking tray lined with baking parchment, and bake them in the oven for 3 minutes on each side. You just want to toast them lightly.
5. Remove them from the oven and let them cool down.
6. Separate the egg whites from the yolks, discard one egg white and place the whites and yolks in different bowls.
7. Whisk the yolks with the sugar until you get a light, pale mousse.
8. Add the mascarpone and whisk at a low speed until creamy.
9. Beat the egg whites into firm peaks.
10. Gently fold the egg whites into the yolk mixture with slow circular movements.
11. Fill a large piping bag with the mascarpone mousse.

My mum's name is Severa Soddu. When I was a child, people used to ask "Is your mum really severa?" Severa means 'strict' in Italian, and I must say she's not strict at all. She's quite chilled as mums go, unless you make a mess of her kitchen. My mum has successfully brought up five children, three boys and two girls, all born in the space of eight years. By successfully I mean that none of us has become a delinquent. When we were very young, my grandmother came to live with us, to give a hand, as my dad used to work very long hours. It was a very busy and lively household. My mum is a pensioner now, so she can relax a little. She loves to read; there's always a book on her kitchen table or on her chair by the fireplace. She adores watching crime dramas and foreign soap operas. She spends her free time visiting friends and family. She's also involved in the local parish with various activities such as helping the poor, the sick and the old people. Her favourite dessert is ricotta cake.

12. Squeeze the oranges and place the juice into a bowl.
13. Line up the cups next to the bowl and dip the panettone circles into the orange juice. Let them soak enough to become moist but not soggy. Place one circle at the bottom of each cup.
14. Take the piping bag and squeeze a layer of mousse over the panettone.
15. Place another circle of panettone dipped in orange juice on top of the mousse.
16. Squeeze another layer of mascarpone mousse on top.
17. Repeat with a third layer of panettone dipped in orange juice.
18. Finish with a layer of mousse at the top.
19. Sprinkle some grated plain chocolate on the mousse.
20. Refrigerate for at least four hours before serving.

Brunella's Tiramisu Coffee

Brunella is addicted to coffee and she loves tiramisu, so she came up with a drinkable version of this dessert. Basically, it's a normal mascarpone mousse 'diluted' with a little milk. You should make it ahead and place it in the fridge for several hours, before serving it with coffee.

1. Separate the egg whites from the yolks and place them in different bowls.
2. Whisk the yolks with the sugar until you get a light, pale mousse.
3. Add the mascarpone and whisk at a low speed until creamy.
4. Add the milk and mix with a spoon.
5. Beat the egg whites into firm peaks.
6. Gently fold the egg whites into the mixture with slow circular movements.
7. You will obtain a mousse which is thinner than your normal mascarpone mousse; it is actually drinkable. If you like it even more liquid, you could add a little extra milk.
8. Pour the mousse into a jug and refrigerate for at least four hours.
9. Make 4 espresso coffees; ask your guests how much sugar they want. Let the coffees cool down.
10. Take the mascarpone mousse from the fridge and give it a stir. Take 4 cappuccino cups and fill them three-quarters full with the mousse.
11. Pour 1 espresso coffee over each cup of mousse. You will notice that some coffee will stay afloat, while some will slide down to the bottom.
12. Decorate the top with some whipped cream and cocoa powder, if you wish.

Serves 4

250 g (9 oz) [1 cup] mascarpone
3 eggs
150 g (5 oz) [¾ cup] sugar
90 ml (3 fl oz) [⅓ cup] milk
4 espresso coffees

*Brunella Formentini is my sister-in-law; she's married to my eldest brother, Roberto. They have a daughter and they live near Reggio Emilia, in Castelnovo nè Monti, a beautiful town on the Appennino Tosco-Emiliano. Brunella works as an administrator in the local hospital, but as soon as she has the opportunity you will see her taking a long walk in the beautiful parks and forests that surround her home. Brunella makes a wonderful chocolate cake; if I ever do a book on Italian cakes, that will have to go in there! She loves reading newspapers, magazines and books, and she has a passion for collecting stamps and nativity sets from all over the world.
Her favourite dessert is apple cake.*

Cristina's Vegan Tiramisu

Serves 4

Ingredients for the vegan sponge cake
150 g (5 oz) [1 dip-and-sweep cup] flour
(plain white flour/unbleached all purpose flour)
2 teaspoons baking powder
90 g (3 oz) [½ cup] brown or white sugar
60 ml (2 oz) [¼ cup] sunflower oil
125 ml (4 fl oz) [½ cup] water
Zest of 1 organic lemon

Making the vegan sponge cake
1. Line the tin with baking parchment. Cristina used a tin measuring 20 cm (8 inches) in diameter.
2. Place the sugar, water, lemon zest and oil in a bowl and mix together well.
3. Sieve the flour and the baking powder and stir.
4. Pour the mixture into the cake tin. Bake in a preheated oven 180°C (350° F) [Gas Mark 4] for 25 minutes or until ready. You can check if your cake is ready by inserting a thin skewer in the middle. If it comes out clean, your cake is done.

Making the vegan mousse
1. Sieve the flour, the sugar and the turmeric into a bowl and mix them well.
2. Put the soya milk with the vanilla extract into a saucepan and bring to the boil.
3. Turn the heat to the minimum and gently add the sieved flour/sugar/turmeric. Whisk well, making sure that no lumps are formed. It's better to use a whisk rather than a spoon for this.
4. Carry on whisking until the milk reaches the consistency of thick custard. Remove from the heat and turn the gas off.
5. Add the soya cream and whisk until you reach a smooth consistency. Your vegan mousse is ready; let it cool down.

Putting it all together
1. Cristina served this tiramisu in cups, but you can use a serving dish or bowls. Cut the sponge cake in 1½ cm (½ inch) wide strips, the thickness of a sponge finger. If you use cups, you can adjust the length of the strips to fit the size of the cups. Place some of the strips at the bottom.
2. Pour some coffee over the strips of cake, enough for them to become moist but not soggy.

My friend Cristina Garau works with her mum in their family-run patisserie, in Gonnosfanadiga, a town north of Cagliari. As well as being passionate about cakes and pastries, Cristina has various hobbies; in particular she's a member of the local drama group and she's active in the Sardinian folk dancing community.

As soon as she has the opportunity and the weather is good, she grabs a book and she leaves at dawn to go to the beach, where she relaxes for half a day. Her parents have a cottage in the countryside, so she occasionally spends her afternoons there with the animals, her dog and cat. Cristina is planning to buy her first property, ideally with a large garden so that she can look after the stray animals that she often finds on the road. Her dream is to be able to go horse riding like she used to when she was younger. She also hopes to find her Prince Charming soon; if he comes along riding a horse, that's a bonus. Her favourite dessert is crème brûlée.

3. Spread a layer of the vegan mousse over the strips of cake.
4. Place the remaining coffee in a bowl and dip your cake strips in it. Unlike sponge fingers, sponge cake absorbs the liquid very quickly, so you have to dip it in and out, otherwise it will disintegrate in the bowl.
5. Place more strips of sponge cake dipped in coffee over the vegan mousse, forming a second layer.
6. Spread another layer of vegan mousse over the cake strips.
7. Depending on the size of your cups/bowls, you may be able to have a third layer of cake and mousse.
8. Finish off with a dusting of cocoa powder over the vegan mousse.
9. Your dessert is ready to be eaten, but if you prefer it cold like a normal tiramisu, I recommend you place it in the fridge for at least two hours.

Ingredients for the mousse and dipping

250 ml (9 fl oz) [1 cup] soya milk
75 g (2½ oz) [6 tablespoons] brown or white sugar
40 g (1½ oz) [⅓ dip-and-sweep cup] flour
(plain white flour/unbleached all purpose flour)
125 ml (4 fl oz) [½ cup] soya cream
1½ teaspoons vanilla extract
Small pinch of turmeric
300 ml (½ pint) [1¼ cups] espresso coffee
Unsweetened cocoa powder

TIRAMISU
DISASTERS

The desserts shown in the photos in this book look appealing, but it wasn't always easy. There have been a few ugly ducklings on the way, and the reason I have included this section in the book is because I think it's important to remind ourselves that the path to success is dotted with occasional failures. I believe that we learn more from our mistakes than from the things that we get right in life, so if you do try any of the recipes in this book and they don't come out as expected, don't feel too bad. Don't give up; just try again. Here are a few disasters for you.

Gluten-free sponge

Here's my first attempt at the gluten-free sponge cake. As you can see, it doesn't look much like a sponge. I could be kind to myself and say it looks like a dry biscuit base, but dry doesn't even cover it. There is no word in the dictionary for it. We had a drought in Sardinia during 2002–2003, where it didn't rain for many months, and that cake crust reminds me of what the soil in my dad's orchard looked like. Just out of curiosity, I dipped a piece in coffee and it dissolved. Try and use that for your tiramisu.

What did I do wrong? Instead of slowly adding the gluten-free flour and mixing it with a wooden spoon, I added it in one go and whisked it with an electric mixer. I should have known better. Then I poured the mixture into a baking tin that was far too large. Two mistakes. Did I mention that I'm no chef?

Moral of the story: when you bake a sponge cake and add the flour to the egg mixture, don't whisk it with an electric mixer, but stir it with a wooden spoon. Also, use a tin of the right dimensions for the amount of mixture.

Tiramisu cheesecake

This was my friend Dalia's first attempt at making a tiramisu cheesecake. She succeeded in making a delicious one (the recipe is in this book), but her first effort was thwarted when she didn't use enough gelatine. She assures me that, despite its looks, this one tasted delicious, and I have no reason to doubt her.

Moral of the story: when you use gelatine, it's very important to follow the instructions on the packet, as each brand will work differently.

Chocolate Tiramisu

You've melted your plain chocolate. You've just added it to the mascarpone mousse. You've stirred it with a wooden spoon and noticed a couple of tiny lumps. Big deal. But then you spot, on your right, still there from before, your electric mixer. Why not use that powerful tool to give it a whisk and make the mousse nice and smooth?
But if you're a little accident-prone, watch out for that plug when you finish. And then ask yourself, was it really necessary to remove every lump?
Moral of the story: a couple of tiny lumps in a mousse are hardly noticeable, especially once the sponge fingers are smothered in it. The problem was non-existent.

Floppy Tiramisu

OK, this is how it goes. You have a baby and you gain a few extra pounds. The baby keeps you awake at night and you crave sleep; you also crave desserts. You try not to have too many sweet things because you want to lose those extra pounds, but in the end you give in and make a tiramisu just to cheer yourself up. Because you're trying to be good you go for the healthier option: you buy low-fat mascarpone.

But there's a problem: the low-fat mascarpone produces a thinner mousse. It doesn't say that on the packet. How are you going to deal with that? You can't think straight because you haven't had enough sleep, but you'd better get on with it before the baby starts screaming again. You add some egg whites. Oh no! For some reason the mousse is even thinner now. Look, it doesn't stay on the sponge fingers. It's rolling off the edges of the dish. What's going to happen when you serve it? Maybe it won't be so bad; perhaps it will set properly once it's been in the fridge for a few hours. Yeah... right.

Moral of the story: do not use low-fat mascarpone for your tiramisu. If you want to go for a healthier option, try the tiramisu light recipe by Claudia. If your mousse turns out too thin, get some whipping cream from the fridge, beat it into stiff peaks and gently add it to the mousse. That should do the trick.

TIRAMISU PARTY

Throw the ultimate Tiramisu Party

It sounds a bit crazy, doesn't it? A tiramisu party. What can you expect? Is it about making tiramisu? Is it about celebrating this wonderful dessert? Is it going to be a gathering of people who just sit there all day and all they do is eat tiramisu? Is there going to be music? And dancing? And fun?

Well, it's your party so you can do whatever you want. All I can offer are some ideas for a party, which, hopefully, will help make it a success.

Idea N⁰ 1
The Invitation

What's the first thing you do when you organize a party? You send out the invitations. It's nice if the invitation is related to the party theme; hence, in this case, a tiramisu party invite. My talented designer Janet has created the ultimate tiramisu party invitation, in case you ever need it, and it can be personalized with your own details. You can download it for free from my website, by subscribing to my newsletter, on www.martinamunzittu.com.

Idea № 2
Tiramisu Buffet

Depending on whether your guests are all adults or a mix of adults and children, I recommend you pick half a dozen tiramisu recipes from this book and prepare the desserts some time before the party. I offer some suggestions about planning later on. You may want to set the tiramisus for adults apart from those for the children, in case some have alcohol in them. Clearly label all desserts.

If you have the time, it may be useful to prepare the tiramisus in single servings, as sometimes people are quite messy when they help themselves from a large serving dish. It's especially easier for children to have their portions already served in smaller paper/plastic cups.

Idea N° 3
Make your own Tiramisu

Imagine the salad bar in a restaurant, where you go and make up your own salad. Well, it's the same idea, but with tiramisu instead. You could have a table laid out with the following: a large bowl with the mascarpone mousse and a serving spoon, a plate with the sponge fingers and several bowls with different types of fruit already cut in small pieces (strawberries, pineapple, banana, peaches, apricots, raspberries, etc.). Then you will have various small containers with grated chocolate, tiny fruit gums, marshmallows, chocolate buttons, etc.
There could be two bowls with different fruit juices, and one bowl with coffee, to dip your sponge fingers in.

Guests can grab a plate and dip the biscuits in the liquid of their choice, before adding their mascarpone mousse on top. They can then add the fruit they would like, if they want a fruity tiramisu, or just add the sprinkled chocolate if they've gone for the coffee flavour. Parents can decorate their children's tiramisus with chocolate buttons, marshmallows or fruit gums, or sprinkle them with chocolate. You can go for seconds if you wish, and try a different flavoured tiramisu.

Idea N⁰ 4
Savoury Counter

I know, this is a tiramisu party, but I strongly recommend you have some savoury stuff to eat as well, as you can feel quite sick if you just have tiramisu. If you want to have an Italian themed party (since tiramisu is Italian), you could buy a few pizzas, ciabattas, garlic bread, focaccias, etc., heat them up in the oven and serve them on a separate table.

Idea № 5
Party bags

Usually party bags are for children, but what about a single party bag, in this case a small box which contains a tiramisu cupcake? Your guests will love to be given a present when they go away. The recipe is in this book and you can buy the boxes in most supermarkets these days. Here are some examples of single cupcake boxes I was able to purchase. If you have the time and patience, you could even make them yourselves (the boxes, I mean. I always meant you to make the cupcakes…).

Idea № 6
Tiramisu Quiz

Why not have a party quiz? You could test the knowledge of your guests when it comes to tiramisu, and offer a prize for the person who gets the most answers right. You can decide in advance what the prize will be. Why not make a tiramisu cake for the winner to take home? Or gift them a copy of this book?

Party quiz

1. What does the word tiramisu mean?

a) get me up

b) pick me up

c) hold me up

2. What is the main dairy ingredient of tiramisu?

a) whipped cream

b) ricotta cheese

c) mascarpone cheese

3. How many layers of sponge fingers and mousse are there in a tiramisu?

a) one of mousse and one of sponge fingers

b) however many layers you want

c) two of mousse and two of sponge fingers

4. How do you handle egg yolks in a tiramisu?

a) you beat them raw with sugar, then add mascarpone

b) you beat them with sugar, add mascarpone and cook on a low heat

c) you mix them with mascarpone and sugar at the same time, then cook on a low heat

5. How long do you dip sponge fingers in coffee before you layer them on the mousse?

a) in and out – less than two seconds

b) give them a good old soak – almost to breaking point

c) put them in and quickly turn them around two or three times

6. What do you sprinkle on top of a classic tiramisu?

a) marshmallows

b) cocoa powder

c) sliced strawberries

7. Where was tiramisu first created?

a) Spain

b) Italy

c) France

8. In which century was tiramisu invented?

a) sixteenth

b) eighteenth

c) twentieth

9. Which tiramisu recipe is the one most people look for on the internet?

a) traditional tiramisu

b) tiramisu cheesecake

c) tiramisu cake

10. What type of coffee do you use to dip your sponge fingers in for your tiramisu?

a) espresso

b) cappuccino

c) latte

These are the correct answers to the quiz.
1 b - 2 c - 3 b - 4 a - 5 c - 6 b - 7 b - 8 c - 9 c - 10 a

Practical notes

Food safety: please remember that your tiramisus will need to be kept cool. I suggest that you get loads of ice, and I mean loads, and seal it inside various plastic bags. Try to flatten the bags so that you get a smooth surface, then place them on your serving tables. You don't need to form a very thick layer, but what is important is that your bags are sealed, so that water doesn't leak out. Alternatively you need plenty of ice packs, enough to cover your tables. Conceal the bags with your tablecloth and there you have it: a cold surface where you will place your tiramisus. It should stay cool for several hours.
I also recommend that you don't take all the desserts out of your fridge at once, but take them as needed. That way they are only exposed to room temperature for as little time as necessary.

Planning: as I mentioned at the beginning of this book, in a fridge tiramisu will keep for three days, so you don't have to go mad trying to do everything at the last minute. If your party is on Saturday evening, for instance, you could make your tiramisus the day before: you could prepare some on Friday morning and some on Friday afternoon. If you have opted for the party boxes, you could make your cupcakes on the Thursday and they would last until Saturday. That would free up your Saturday morning to get the party room ready with decorations, and for last-minute preparations. You might even be able to make another tiramisu that morning, if you realize you don't have enough desserts. Another issue, and this is not trivial, is making space in your fridge to store all these tiramisus, as it's of paramount importance that they are kept cool. Imagine preparing two tiramisus and then realizing that there's no room in your fridge. That's the last nightmare you want to face when organizing a party. So, before you even start, think in advance about how much space you have in your fridge, how many tiramisus you can store and what to do if there isn't enough room. Perhaps you can borrow some space in your neighbour's fridge for the occasion.

Final notes for your tiramisu party

There are many details that will help a party be successful. The entertainment is an important factor. Don't forget to have some music playing – if you can get your hands on some Italian pop songs, all the better. The entertainment also depends on whether there are children, and so do the decorations. I won't go into details such as drinks, as these will vary for every party and will depend on the people invited. Ultimately, the success of the party relies on many factors, but the most important one is the people: how much fun they intend to have.

Here's a final check-list that might prove useful for your party

1. Set the date
2. Make a list of who to invite
3. Send the invitations
4. Arrange entertainment, music
5. Check who has replied
6. Work out the final numbers
7. Decide which tiramisu you're going to make and draft a shopping list
8. Add other items to your shopping list; for example: savoury foods, drinks, paper plates, plastic cutlery, napkins, cups, decorations and ice
9. Make a plan of when you will prepare the various tiramisus; plan for the occasional thing to go wrong and allow for extra time
10. Do the shopping
11. Prepare the tiramisus
12. Hang party decorations/set room up
13. Prepare party bags/boxes
14. Welcome guests
15. Have fun

Acknowledgements

This book would not exist if it weren't for my friends and family who contributed the delicious recipes that are featured here. So my first thank you goes out to them. I wanted to share with you the name of each person who created a scrumptious dessert, and tell you a little bit about them after their recipe. I think that somehow we put a little bit of ourselves in everything we create, and maybe when you make a tiramisu from one of these recipes, it will feel like you have got to know one of my friends or family a little bit as well.

One of the biggest challenges for me, when I was writing the quantities of the ingredients, was the measurement conversion. I am Italian and I think in metric. I have lived in the UK for several years, and have just about got the hang of the imperial system. Now I have discovered American cups – another entity that, up to a few months ago, I thought was a simple kitchen cup; but hey no, it is actually a measure in its own right, and apparently gets used for both volume and weight, to make matters more complicated for someone like me. I felt like I had been thrown in at the deep end, until I found a very nice and knowledgeable food blogger and freelance writer (print and web), Jean, from www.delightfulrepast.com, who was extremely helpful and gave me some great advice on converting my metric measurements to US cups. So a massive thank you goes to Jean.

Another challenge was arranging the photos for my book. Having written fiction before, I had never handled images and text together, so I needed some help with that. And there I found Janet Tallon, a very talented designer who was able to create a great looking cookery book, a fantastic cover and an enticing tiramisu party invitation.

And last but not least, the final polish to the manuscript came from Jude White, an exceptional proofreader.

About Martina Munzittu

I was born and raised in Italy (Sardinia); I now live in Cambridgeshire, UK, with my husband and young daughter. I write contemporary romance and chick-lit books. My debut novel *A Deal with a Stranger* is a romantic/mystery set in Sardinia; *Incompatible Twins* and *The Broken Heart Refuge* are set in London.

Like many Italians, I have a passion for food and this comes across in my books, where the Italian protagonists of my stories are often obsessed with cooking and eating.

My latest books are dedicated to this passion: *Tiramisu Recipes from Italian Friends and Family* is the first of three, soon to be followed by *Pasta Sauce Recipes* and *Risotto Recipes*. All my cookery books follow the same format, which is a collection of recipes and photos from my family and friends from Italy.

To learn more visit www.martinamunzittu.com where you can subscribe to my newsletter and hear about new releases, giveaways and special promotions. You can also download and personalize your free tiramisu party invitation.

Index

A

Alcohol **7, 80**
    Baileys **7, 50**
    Cointreau **7, 34, 42**
    Limoncello **14**
    Martini **46**
    Rum **32**
Almonds **16**

B

Baileys **50**
Bananas **31**
Biscuits **16, 29, 48, 56**
Brownie Tiramisu **37–38**

C

Cakes **20–23, 26, 39–41**
Cheesecake **29, 38, 70**
Children's Recipes **20–25, 39–42, 58**
Chocolate **7**
Chocolate Brownie **37–38**
Chocolate Tiramisu **46, 72**
Cocoa Powder **7**
Coconut **19**
Coffee **7, 63**
Cointreau **7, 34, 42**
Cupcakes **26**

D

Dipping Liquids **6–7**
    See also alcohol

E

Egg Whites **6**
Eggs **6**
Espresso **7**

F

Food Safety **6, 92**
Freezing **8**
Fruit
    Bananas **31**
    Coconut **19**
    Juice **7**
    Lemons **14, 16, 31, 48**
    Oranges **34, 60–61**
    Peaches **56**
    Pineapple **32**

G

Gelatine **29**
Gelato **53**
Gluten-Free **54–55, 68**

H

Hazelnuts **31**
History **5**

I

Ice Cream Tiramisu **53**

L

Lady Fingers **6**
Lemon **14, 16, 31, 48**
Lemon Curd **48**
Light Tiramisu **16**
Limoncello **14**
Liquids, For Dipping **6–7**
    See also alcohol
Low-Fat Tiramisu **16, 74**
Low-Sugar Tiramisu **16**

M

Martini **46**
Mascarpone **6**
    Problems with **8, 74**

N

Nuts **16, 31**

O

Oranges **34, 60–61**

P

Pancakes **44**
Panettone **60–61**
Party Invitations **78–79**
Peaches **56**
Pineapple **32**

Q

Quiz **88–89**

R

Refrigeration **8, 9**
Ricotta **16**
Rum **32**

S

Shortbread **48, 56**
Sponge Cake **6**
Sponge Fingers **6, 8–9**
Stevia **16**
Strawberries **42**
Sugar **7**
    alternative to **16**

T

Tools And Equipment **9**
Traditional Tiramisu **12**

V

Vegan Tiramisu **64–65**